Selina Lake
WINTER LIVING STYLE

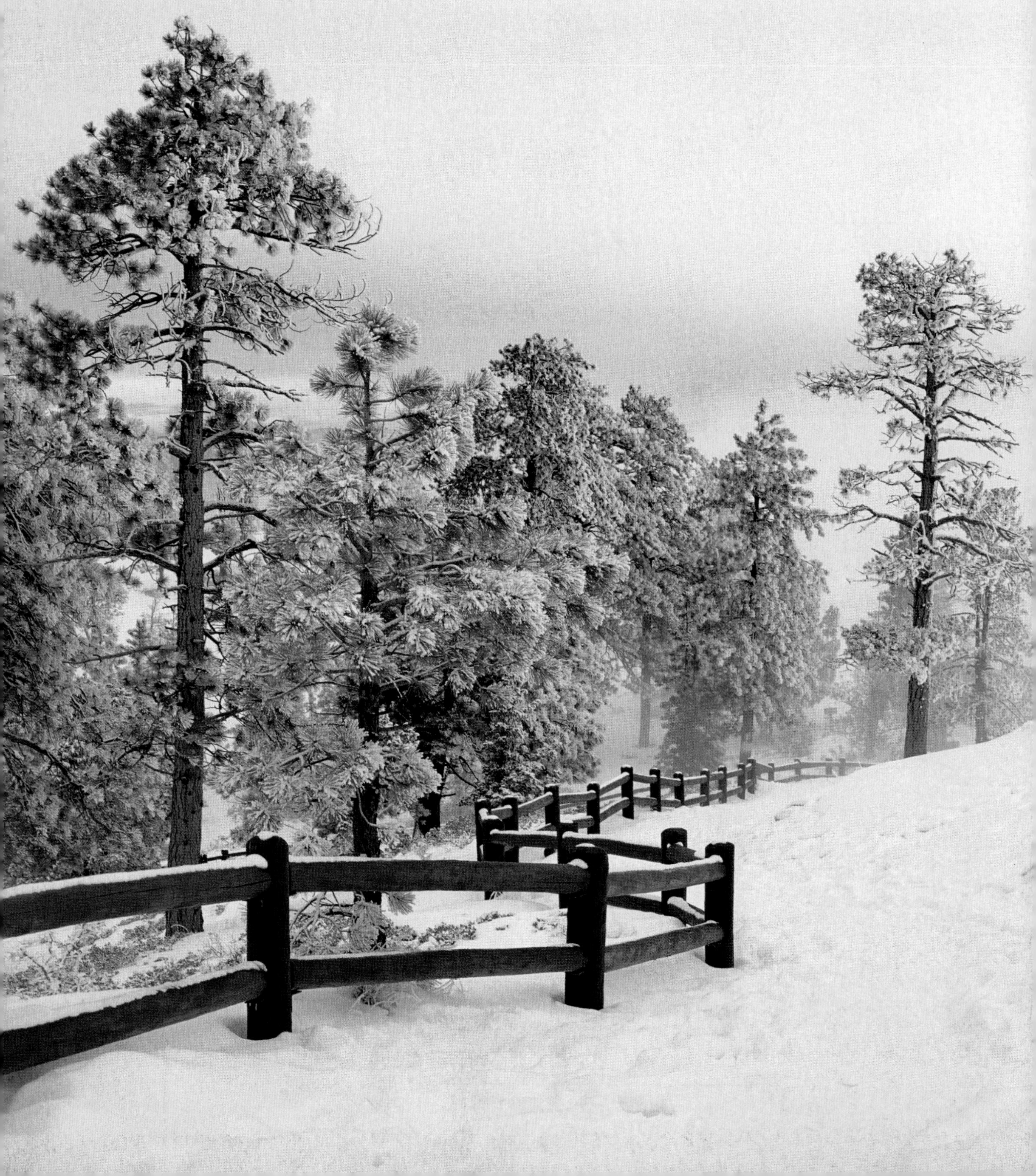

Selina Lake
WINTER LIVING STYLE

BRING HYGGE INTO YOUR HOME WITH THIS INSPIRATIONAL GUIDE TO DECORATING FOR WINTER

PHOTOGRAPHY BY **DEBI TRELOAR**

RYLAND PETERS & SMALL
LONDON • NEW YORK

Senior Designer
Megan Smith
Commissioning Editor
Annabel Morgan
Head of Production
Patricia Harrington
Art Director
Leslie Harrington
Editorial Director
Julia Charles
Publisher
Cindy Richards

Indexer
Vanessa Bird

First published in 2015
as *Winter Living*.
This revised edition
published in 2020 by
Ryland Peters & Small
20–21 Jockey's Fields,
London WC1R 4BW
and
341 E 116th St
New York, NY 10029
www.rylandpeters.com

Text © Selina Lake
2015, 2020

Design and photographs ©
Ryland Peters & Small
2015, 2020

ISBN 978 1 78879 243 1

Printed and bound in China

10 9 8 7 6 5 4 3 2 1

A CIP record for this
book is available from the
British Library. US Library
of Congress Cataloging-in-
Publication Data has been
applied for.

Contents

Introduction 6

Winter INSPIRATIONS 8

Homespun CHARM 38

Faded GRANDEUR 62

Rustic RETREAT 86

Winter WHITES 110

Festive CELEBRATIONS 134

SOURCES 154   BUSINESS CREDITS 157

INDEX 158   ACKNOWLEDGMENTS 160

Introduction

There's something truly magical about winter. It's the time of year that makes us want to nest – to make our homes feel cosy and snug – and welcome friends and family at festive parties and gatherings. In this book I share my tips for styling and decorating the home in order to create lovely, uplifting interiors during the winter months. It starts with my 'Winter Inspirations', which is full of ideas for putting together dramatic winter floral displays, wallpaper and fabrics. Then in each chapter I explore a different style theme: 'Homespun', 'Faded Grandeur', 'Rustic' and 'Winter Whites', all of which will hopefully inspire you. The concluding chapter is 'Festive Celebrations', in which you'll discover how I style my own home ready for Christmas, featuring ideas on how to create country, natural and traditional looks. I also show you how to put together a colour-pop party and a romantic soirée for New Year's Eve in a gorgeous old barn. I love getting crafty and making my own decorations and textiles, so throughout the book follow my 'Makes' and have a go at making your own lampshade garland, simple cushions/pillows or pinecone firelighters. I hope you have fun getting your home ready for the winter magic.

There's a lot to inspire us in winter.
I love the magical feeling you get
when you wake up to a blanket of snow
outside. The sun is lower in winter,
which can create a glorious golden light
in the evenings and shadows that are
long and deep. Over the next few pages
I share what I like to get up to during
the winter months and show you how
to style your home to make the most
of this wonderful season.

Winter INSPIRATIONS

The joy of WINWINTER

✳ Styling my home with twinkling tealights on the mantelpiece, cosy blankets thrown over the back of the sofa, snuggly faux-fur rugs on the floor by the bedside and piles of vintage eiderdowns adorning the bed. ✳ Drinking cups of steaming hot chocolate/cocoa, while sitting inside by a roaring fire. ✳ Heading out for long winter walks in the countryside with my family, wrapped up with woolly hats, scarves and gloves. ✳ Crafting away the long, dark afternoons and early evenings. ✳ Venturing into the cold to forage in the garden for berries and foliage to make winter posies. ✳ The build-up to the festive celebrations and bringing my collection of vintage Christmas baubles down from the attic. ✳ Eating, drinking and making merry!

My top ten things
TO DO IN WINTER

2 getting cosy

When it's cold outside we all want to feel snug and cosy, so make sure you have extra blankets and throws ready. I like to layer beds in the winter with a mix of vintage eiderdowns, knitted blankets and quilts for extra warmth. A hot-water bottle is also an essential for keeping cosy. Pop one in your bed 10 minutes before you climb in to get it nice and toasty for you.

1 baking cakes

I like to bake cakes during the winter so I can offer any house guests a slice. One of my favourites is a chocolate fruit and nut bundt cake. I bought my vintage bundt tin/pan from a junk shop and use it all the time. I use a variant of a Victoria sponge recipe, but I substitute some of the flour for cocoa powder, and add dried fruits along with chopped-up milk chocolate and mixed nuts. Once the cake has baked, I remove it to the pan/tin. I love the pretty pattern the tin/pan leaves on the cake. I then decorate the cake with a dusting of icing/confectioners' sugar and display it on a vintage glass cake stand.

3 roaring fires & toasting marshmallows

Having an open fire is a real luxury and will not only keep your room warm and welcoming, but it will also be a focal point. The fireplaces in our Victorian house had been covered up by the previous owners, so when we moved in we got to work reinstating the openings. We bought original Victorian marble fireplace surrounds from eBay, which my husband installed in our living room (see page 138). A perfect winter afternoon for us is sitting in front of the fire, drinking hot chocolate/cocoa and toasting marshmallows.

4 getting crafty & learning a new skill

Winter is the perfect time to take up a new crafting hobby because, let's face it, it's probably too cold for most outdoor activities. Why not invest in a new craft book or search for how-to guides on the Internet. I love getting crafty when winter is approaching, particularly making my own Christmas cards. I also make some of my presents for my friends and family. This winter I'm going to try and learn more sewing techniques so I can jump back on my sewing machine. I'm also going to finish knitting the scarf I started last year.

6 throwing a winter party

I love arranging parties at any time of the year because it's a great excuse to do some party styling. For a winter dinner party, candles are a must to add a bit of magic to the table, with vases of richly coloured winter flowers scattered in between. I always serve drinks to match the season, so I make batches of warm mulled wine and mulled cider, which I serve in tall vintage glasses with stripey straws. I like to decorate the space with festoon lights, electric-pink honeycomb pom-poms and a mass of twinkling tealights.

5 winterizing the home

The beginning of autumn is the perfect time to get your home ready for the winter months to follow. Perhaps you could replace light voile curtains with thicker lined window treatments. You might want to have a change-around with your accessories, such as taking out a pastel- or light-coloured cushion/pillow and replacing it with something richer and darker. Fill tealight holders and lanterns with candles ready for the early dark evenings and change your bedding from cool, light and airy to warm, woolly and layered.

7 wrapping gifts

Each Christmas I like to come up with a different wrapping theme for my gifts. One year I wrapped all the presents I'd bought or made for my friends and family in vintage-style floral wallpapers, which I decorated with a mixture of pinks ribbons and bows. I like to come up with my theme early so I've got plenty of time to shop for the items I need, such as ribbons, papers and name tags in the right style. This year I'm going to my local do-it-yourself store to buy off-white lining wallpaper (it's much cheaper than actual gift wrap). I'll then decorate the wrapped presents with neon-pink ribbon and home-made gold glitter tags.

8 decorating with my vintage bauble collection

I've been collecting vintage tree ornaments for years, and I search charity shops and flea markets looking for these pretty handprinted glass baubles throughout the year. I use them to decorate our Christmas Tree in the living room (see page 138). Any leftover decorations will adorn the mantelpiece, or I'll arrange them in glass jars and on vintage plates.

9 making my own christmas cards

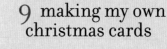

I always make my close family and friends handmade cards, but I also buy handmade cards from craft fairs and shops. I buy packs of A4/US Letter white card and cut each sheet in half twice to get the right size. I sometimes use stamps, hand-drawn motifs, photocopied photographs or collage papers to decorate them. I also love receiving handmade cards!

10 making a wreath

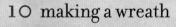

I love hanging a handmade wreath on our front door in the run-up to the festive period. I use a metal wreath frame and then weave cuttings from the evergreen plants in our garden to bulk out the round shape. Once the entire frame is covered, I add baubles, ribbon bows, woolly pom-poms or flowers and berries, depending on what style I'm going for that year. (See page 136 for my Festive Dress-the-Door tips.)

* I love how a blanket of snow makes everything beautiful and pure - a truly magical scene.

During the winter most of us spend more time indoors, rather than braving the cold for a night out. We'll stay in and invite friends over for dinner or drinks, and have the family over for afternoon tea and gatherings. So it's a good time to think about styling your space.

There are a few practicalities to consider when styling your home for winter: number one is keeping your rooms warm and welcoming. Dig out the blankets and throws you tucked away during the summer

In this Danish wood cabin a sofa has been adorned with Turkish cushions/pillows in dark floral designs (opposite). The armchair has been made inviting with a Mongolian rug, and on the floor is a patchwork of rugs and cushions/pillows. Behind this wood-burning stove hangs a wallpaper panel by Deborah Bowness. The burnt-orange chairs bring in a retro element to the cosy space (below).

Style your home
FOR WINTER

and freshen them up with a quick, cool spin in the washing machine. Once dry, drape them over the arm of your sofa or armchair, lay them on your bed and stack the rest in a pile on a shelf or in basket, so they can be easily grabbed when needed.

Next, think about your flooring. There are painted floorboards in most of the rooms in our house, so I use a large Moroccan-style rug in the living room from The Plantation Rug Company to add warmth. In our bedroom I use faux-fur rugs from IKEA on both sides of our bed, and in the kitchen a woven plastic Moroccan mat works well to keep the draughts at bay, plus it's easy to wipe clean.

There's no need to rush out and buy loads of new furnishings for your home –

for the *Winter Living* style you can work with what you already have and dress it for the season, perhaps investing in a few new accessories. I like to use a mix of chair styles around our dining table and to make them more comfy I add cushions, faux-fur rugs and folded knitted blankets. Sometimes simply arranging a few candles along your dining table or sideboard will make your space feel even more wintery. Use a mix of tealight holders, candlesticks or large pillar candles placed in jars and vases.

Rearranging or adding new artworks and prints is another way to make your space feel ready for winter. Perhaps you could invest in a wintery wallpaper panel from Deborah Bowness, or posters and prints by Fine Little Day. I also love vintage botanical wall charts on dark backgrounds.

Depending on how you have already decorated your home, there are a few different natural elements which can be brought in. Galvanized pots of mini pine trees work well in rustic spaces, whereas dried hydrangeas and deep-pink heathers fit into a faded grandeur theme, and pots or vases of white Amaryllis on a white dining table will work well if you're after a predominantly white theme. I love making arrangements with a mix of colours for crafty, homespun spaces.

Textiles need to be considered at this time of year too. You could swap your summery-print cushions/pillows for dark florals, perhaps in either velvet or knit. Bedding can also be changed from the light and cool covers used in the warmer months to thicker duvets/comforters, eiderdowns and blankets.

The simple, elegant armchair in a Mid-Century Modern-style is from IKEA (above). I added a Mabel and Bird handmade cushion/pillow and a knitted blanket for extra comfort. The pine-cone garland is easy to make: simply spray some pinecones with artificial snow or white paint and tie them onto a length of cord or string decorated with ribbons – I used narrow black satin ribbon. The walls are painted in vintage grey from Valspar and I arranged a mix of waxflower and eucalyptus in the glass jar on the table to add scent to the room (opposite).

✳ Style tip

When we moved into our house, we uncovered this fireplace opening in our dining room, so we decided to install a Malvern ACR woodburning stove, which is brilliant for heating up the entire downstairs. I used Farrow & Ball Pitch Black emulsion/latex paint to paint the brickwork and I dressed the space on either side with stacks of logs, so they are ready to throw into the fire; they also give the fireplace the feel of a log cabin. For added style, make a hand-tied arrangement of winter foliage. Here, I used a branch from a pine tree, eucalyptus and red berries from the garden, and tied them together with some black ribbon.

Winter SCENTS

It's too cold to keep our windows open for very long during the winter when our homes are in need of some fresh air, so it's the ideal time to introduce some warming and fragrant winter scents. Burning incense sticks and sage smudge sticks will certainly add some lovely aromas to your space. Another option is to bring in winter scents from outside – bunches of freshly picked pine sprigs, along with bouquets of rosemary, are a great addition. I also like to introduce bundles of cinnamon sticks and bunches of eucalyptus. For a stylish touch, collect some fallen pinecones and arrange them in an old wooden crate or basket, and spray them with your favourite room freshener. For me, the ultimate winter fragrance comes from scented candles – I can't get enough of them. My favourites are Baies by Diptyque, Moroccan Rose by True Grace and Honey & Amber by Plum & Ashby.

making scents
Smudge sticks are bundles of dried herbs, bound together (below left). They have a history of being used as part of a cleansing ritual or for religious ceremonies. I use sage sticks purely for their essence – I bought these online, but they are quite simple to make yourself. An old drinks crate is the perfect pinecone holder (below centre). A vase of garden pickings brings the scents of a winter garden indoors (below right).

Make clove-studded oranges

Orange pomanders fill the home with a delicious scent and look pretty too. To make them, buy some fresh oranges and cloves from your local market. Simply press the cloves into the oranges, making a pattern as you go. You could choose a random spot pattern or spell out short seasonal words such as Noel. Once you're happy with the design, tie each orange up with ribbon, like you would a parcel, leaving lengths of ribbon to tie a bow. Display them as hanging decorations or arrange on a shelf or tabletop.

Winter FLORALS

In the winter months I am always drawn to strong flower motifs arranged on dark backgrounds. These floral patterns may be woven into rugs or scattered over velvet fabrics and wallpapers. If full-on dark florals feel a little too heavy, you could introduce them into your home in the form of accessories – perhaps a deep-plum lampshade with a dramatic all-over flower pattern, or an oversized cushion/pillow in emerald-green floral-print velvet. I'm planning to line the inside of my wardrobe/closet with a gorgeous, dark, vintage wallpaper, so I get a handsome floral hit every time I open the doors – I just need to find the perfect vintage wallpaper.

dark floral posies

In the summer I love putting together posies of seasonal flowers and using recycled jars as vases to display them in. In the colder months I enjoy creating arrangements from whatever the garden has to offer at this time of year, mixed in with any unusual flower varieties that I find at my local florist. For the arrangements on this page I used a mix of red and yellow berries with antirrhinums and the little yellow pompoms of craspedia (above), and long, hanging silvery catkins of the silk tassel bush, vivid berries and the bright red stems of dogwood (right). White amaryllis are large and stunning, and make a gorgeous seasonal display. I like to buy a few amaryllis bulbs as well as cut stems, which I arrange in tall galvanized-metal buckets (above right).

painterly arrangements

There aren't many flowers growing in my garden here in the UK in the middle of winter – only some red berries that the birds haven't got their beaks onto yet, rose hips, colourful heathers and a few purple Hellebores sheltering under a tree. However, with a little help, that's still plenty to start a beautiful winter floral arrangement – the perfect uplifting remedy for the gloomy weather. When I'm putting together winter florals, I pick whatever I can from the garden and then head to my local florist or favourite flower market to add some more colours and textures. It always surprises me how much choice there is during in winter; yes, admittedly some of the flowers are forced or shipped in, but it's still really exciting to see all these new varieties that are rarely available in the other seasons of the year.

In this old wooden box (opposite far left) I've collected a few leftover sprigs, flower heads, leaves and redcurrants ready to use to make an autumn wreath. A storage jar makes a sweet vase for this orange asclepias (opposite right). I love this vintage pink vase against the amazing Farmhouse Floral limited edition wallpaper by Deborah Bowness (above left). The floral arrangement is a mix of red berries, white and red amaryllis, deep-plum anemones, yellow craspedia pom-poms and very early white lilac. The last arrangement is made up of pale-pink cockscomb (also known as wool flowers, although I think they look more like coral), orange and red berries, sprigs of purple Geraldton waxflower and a few orange Proteas.

Experiment by putting a mix of beautiful blooms together in a vase, jug, crate or jar, and let the colourful arrangement banish the winter blues.

floral wallpapers & fabrics

I'm a huge fan of floral prints, and I'm always drawn to textiles and papers sporting floral motifs. Floral patterns seem an obvious choice for spring and summer, but decorating with flowers can work just as well in the winter. The way to introduce floral patterns into your home at this time of year is to opt for dark florals set on a black canvas – it's all about the moodier palette. Finding vintage floral wallpaper is a joy, and I've been lucky in the past to find untouched rolls in charity and second-hand shops/thrift stores. Retro Villa in Copenhagen sells hundreds of rolls of British papers from the 1950s, 1960s and 1970s both in the shop and online. I also love the floral wallpapers by Deborah Bowness and Cole & Son.

_* *Style tip*

I used this gorgeous Nostalgic Blossom wallpaper mural by Mr Perswall for the wall behind our bed – it looks rich and thick enough to be a fabric covering. I kept the rest of room neutral to avoid floral overload, as I wanted the space to be calm and sleep-enhancing. I chose light-grey linen bedding and white pillows so the wallpaper is the main focus.

changing seasons

Hydrangeas (opposite) are extraordinary flowers that just keep on giving, all year long. In the summer we are wowed by their impressive blooms and colours, which range from delicate pinks and greens to vibrant pinks, purples and deep blues. Towards the end of summer, pick the last of the flowers from your garden if you grow them; if not, buy yourself a big bunch from a florist. Arrange them in a vase of water and enjoy them until they start to dry out, then empty the water, remove any leaves and place them in a clean, dry vase to let them dry out. Watch the colours change and fade until it becomes a more wintry-looking arrangement.

✳ Original botanical wall charts are stunning but hard to come by. Luckily this 1800s Heather Print has been reproduced by Wallography.

These lovely Turkish woven cushions/ pillows are a great way to introduce winter florals into your living room (below). Their dark and moody design sets the tone for the whole room. Opposite is an original 1970s botanical wall chart of a potato plant in blossom.

berries & boughs

Berries (opposite) are winter's version of spring blossom. Well, for a short time... before the birds have a feast. If you have berries in your garden and want to create a gorgeous display, perhaps on your kitchen or dining table, invest in a pair of decent garden pruners and a pair of gloves, as most plants and trees that produce berries also have sharp thorns. Gather your collection of cuttings and arrange them in large glass jars filled with water. I particularly like using long rose hip cuttings and the beautiful autumnal berries of the callicarpa shrub. Place shorter cuttings of rosemary, ivy and holly in a variety of vases and glass bottles (above right). A windowsill is a great place for a vase of winter pines and berries (above far right). I use pine-scented candles handmade by Honest in collaboration with Cereal magazine alongside arrangements of berries to add to the winter feeling (right). Golden crabapple fruit makes a pretty, stylish touch to this table setting (far right).

Cosy and colourful, this chapter is for those who love to craft and style their home with glorious handmade, second-hand and restored flea-market finds. This style is warm and welcoming, with comfy textiles such as crochet blankets, vintage florals, barkcloth, hand-knitted details and lots of individual touches and uplifting, vibrant pops of bright colour – perfect for winter.

Homespun
CHARM

"LA QUALITÉ FRANÇAISE"   FRANCE

Homespun Charm
TEXTURE & TONES

Rich tones of mustard, vintage browns and burnt orange are blended with bright pops of neon pink, jade and tones of red to create this winter homespun style. Textures are one of the main design features of the homespun look. Hand-knitted items give spaces a cosy, lived-in feel, and home-made details such as crochet-edged pillowcases and hand-painted ceramics add to the eclectic look. Textiles are a mix of faux fur and soft velvets in olive and mustard hues with a rich mix of floral patterns in earthy colours. Beds are layered with vintage eiderdowns, knitted or crocheted blankets and an array of cushions/pillows, and living rooms always feature a collection of blankets and throws ready to snuggle under. Different wooden surfaces bring a natural element into the interior and make a perfect backdrop for the vivid colours. Wooden surfaces are either left natural, or painted in dark tones. Furniture is mix-and-match, and includes finds such as old, worn wooden tables surrounded by a mix of painted or stained wooden chairs of various styles and comfortable, fabric-covered sofas and armchairs.

vintage decorating ideas

I love making vintage arrangements with amaryllis, dark anemones and berries (top left). Colourful balls of wool make a sweet decoration in a large bowl, jar or basket (top centre). A new lampshade has been covered with pretty, vintage fabric, while the base is made from an old French glass bottle (top right). This yellow ceramic egg holder is a good place to store bits and bobs (below left). Old knitted clothes can always be turned into cushion covers if you're handy with a sewing machine (bottom centre). Vintage floral fabrics look lovely piled neatly, ready for the next sewing project (bottom right).

MADE BY HAND

Winter is the perfect month to spend time crafting or taking up a new hobby, as we tend to spend more time huddling indoors. Look out for craft workshops in your area, which provide fantastic opportunities to learn new skills. The homespun look is all about mixing different crafts together and supporting independent designers and makers, so check out local craft markets and be sure to browse through all the wonderful offerings on websites such as Folksy and Etsy. Some stores have also embraced the Homespun movement and celebrate the style by commissioning independent designers to design a capsule collection for them. Anthropologie is a good example of this and offers some great homespun pieces.

I love introducing a couple of vivid tones to a winter homespun scheme. This neon-pink hand-knitted tea cosy gives this country cottage kitchen a real pop of homespun loveliness.

I love this neon-pink knitted tea cosy with its giant pom-pom made by Christian from The People Shop (opposite left). I made this simple envelope-style cushion/pillow cover using Linwood Fabrics Hudson Bay 2 Heather – delightful for making homespun cushions/pillows this winter (opposite right). A coat-hook board has been put up in this wood-clad hallway, painted emerald green, to hang up winter coats and a funky knitted stocking decorated with pom-poms during the festive period (above left). To give the homespun style a wintery feel, look out for items with woodland motifs, such as this deer and hare ceramic plate from Anthropologie (above).

Make a simple cushion cover

You'll need fabric, fabric scissors, a sewing machine, an iron, cushion pad, pins, a measuring tape and ribbon. Measure the pad and add 1.5 cm/½ in. seam allowance to three of the sides and an extra 3.5 cm/ 1½ in. to the bottom. Cut out two pieces to these measurements for the front and back. Sew a hem to the wrong side along the bottom of both sections and stitch in place. Lay the front section down with the right side facing up, then lay the back section on top with the right side facing down. Pin around the three sides, leaving an opening at the bottom. Stitch together, then turn right side out. Sew two lengths of ribbon along the hem edge and two on the other side. Insert the pad and tie the ribbon tabs together creating two bows along the bottom of the cushion.

Make an autumn-leaf garland

To make this lovely seasonal decoration, you'll need a collection of leaves, heather, ribbons and a herb-drying chandelier (the one shown here is from mail-order company Cox and Cox). First, gather together little bundles of leaves and some sprigs of heather, and tie them together with ribbon. I used a mix of natural string and narrow neon-pink ribbon. Loop the ribbon around the hooks on the chandelier and you're done. You could also turn it into a Christmas decroation with winter foliage, berries and baubles.

heavenly homepsun breakfast

I can't imagine anything more delightful than enjoying thick slices of toast and butter with home-made jam/jelly and a cup of delicious blended tea while keeping warm next to an Aga oven in a cosy country kitchen (above left and opposite). I love discovering new teas and I like the idea of storing it in sealed glass canisters with cute labels, rather than a pile of colourful boxes from the supermarket (above). Pretty knitted socks hang in front of the aga to dry while the kettle boils (left), filling the room with the scent of fresh laundry – a heavenly way to start the day.

warm blankets & toasty toes

The furniture in this cosy living space has been positioned around the wood-burning stove, which pumps out heat. Handmade wooden stools make perfect little side tables and the handmade vintage lampshade and giant cushion/pillow add some pretty floral patterns to the scene. The tongue-and-groove walls are painted in a soft white-grey.

scandi homespun

When creating a Scandi look, one of the key elements is wood cladding.

Even if you decide to clad just one room, you'll instantly introduce a Scandinavian feel to the space. The Scandi homespun look is simplistic and mixes utility with beauty. Walls and flooring tend to be white, or versions of white and soft grey, and colour is added to the space with accessories. Furniture is a mix of simple new designs and traditional handcrafted pieces made from wood, with comfy fabric-covered sofas and armchairs piled with a combination of velvet and linen cushions/pillows. This style is a blend of craft and cool.

The metal-frame windows have not been cluttered by window dressings, so you don't miss out on the lovely country views. The only decoration comes from a simple garland draped across the window (above left). It is made from leaves that have been painted white and then attached to a length of string, with the occasional leaf left unpainted. This lamp (above right) has been made by hand using vintage floral fabric for the shade, an old glass bottle for the base and a table lamp kit, which includes the light fitting and flex.

Make a chandelier decoration

To make this lovely decoration (below), you'll need a chandelier, old bulbs (the ones below were used in old street lamps in the north of England, which adds character, charm and a sense of history), either in the same style or in a variety of different shapes and sizes, some sprigs of foliage and ribbons of different colours and widths. Choose your desired length and style of ribbon, and tie a knot around the base of each bulb, making sure to trap a sprig or two of foliage beneath the ribbon. Carefully loop the ribbon over one of the arms of the chandelier. If you don't have a chandelier, you could alternatively hang them in a cluster from the end of a curtain pole or on coat hooks.

* Style tip

Make homespun arrangements of flowers and foliage to add some splashes of colour along a windowsill (above). Collect glass bottles, jars and glasses in a mix of sizes – amber-coloured glass will give the windowsill a lovely warm glow. Fill the jars and bottles with fresh water and arrange sprigs of berries, dark-coloured Snapdragon flowers and small branches of autumn leaves. Also, check out the vintage paper pendant lampshades (opposite), made by cutting circles out of old books and sticking them onto a large paper lantern to make a fish-scale pattern. I also love the mix-and-match chairs grouped around the modern Scandi-style trestle table.

✻ I love these traditional Norwegian patterned hand-knitted socks and mittens.

All of this adorable knitwear hanging on these clotheslines has been hand-knitted by the grandmother of one of the owners of this beautiful house. An indoor washing line is a highly practical idea in really cold countries, where you could be waiting sometime for washing to dry outside! You could buy a fancy clothes airer suspended from the ceiling on a pulley, or simply screw in hooks and string up a clothesline or two. Hanging them above a wood-burning stove, if you have one, would be an ideal spot.

cosy cabins

If someone mentions 'log cabin' to me, an image immediately pops into my head of an inviting wood-clad building, with a open fire or log burner surrounded by a couple of comfy armchairs covered in blankets and a snug rug on the floor. Add a warming mug of hot chocolate/cocoa and you have the recipe for bliss.

If you have been lucky enough to enjoy holidays/vacations or long weekends in a log cabin, you might have already been seduced by their many charms. I love their quirky structures and intimate spaces, but even more than that I adore the feeling of being surrounded by nature — not something that city and town dwellers experience that much. We often hire log cabins to escape for a few days with our loved ones.

The built-in cupboards in this cabin kitchen (below left) were recycled and remoulded to fit the unusual space. The poster is from Fine Little Day. Behind this wood-burning hangs a Deborah Bowness Christmas Tree wallpaper panel (below). A velvet swivel chair brings in a Mid-Century Modern element.

a riot of homspun colour
The beautiful vintage floral-patterned curtains/drapes, with their pink background and pink-and-yellow trim, make a vibrant statement (opposite). The bed is dressed with a pure-cotton duvet/comforter cover and a vintage floral pom-pom trimmed throw adds a layer of warmth. In true homespun style, the pillowcases don't match – a mock toile in black is teamed with a white pillowcase with yellow embroidered trim. The walls have been painted white to offset the abundance of colour in the room. The metal bed (right) is dressed with beautiful linen covers from The Linen Works, in a mix of soft greys. Then I layered the bed it with a dusky-pink quilt from Cox and Cox and a collection of dusky-pink cushions/pillows. The Anthropologie throw, with dashes of neon-pink, gives the room a homespun pop of colour.

snug bedrooms

It's pretty easy to make homespun bedrooms snug and cosy when the temperatures drop – you need lots of layers, a thick duvet/comforter and a mountain of cushions/pillows. I like to use linen or cotton duvet/comforter covers and pillowcases in natural colours, and build up warmth and colour by layering colourful blankets and throws. Include bedding with pretty details like crochet trims, pom-pom edging and cushions/pillows with fluffy fringes. Thick, vintage fabric curtains will add personality to the room and will help to keep out any draughts. Keep the main lighting soft by using vintage floral lampshades. Anglepoise-style lamps work well by bedsides.

Rainbow-coloured crocheted blankets can be used to add a little colour and charm to any space (right), draped over an arm of a chair, piled in a basket or simply stacked on a shelf or chair. I buy handmade crocheted blankets in second-hand/thrift shops; after a couple of cool washes in the washing machine they are ready to be used. Make your own pom-pom garlands to decorate your bedroom (below) – they are so easy to make.

calm yet colourful

The feature in this homespun bedroom (opposite) is the vibrant yellow-painted celling, which has been painted right down to the picture rail. It's a great way to bring in some colour, while still keeping the space calm. The headboard has been covered in a natural linen and the bed dressed with white cotton sheets, while gorgeous vintage floral cushions/pillows add to the charm. A multi-coloured crocheted blanket adds an extra layer of warmth and ties in with the colourful ceiling. The lampshade has been covered in old, folded newspaper, and a vase of winter flowers and berries has been positioned on the bedside table. Above the bed, individual printed letters that spell out 'You & Me' have been stuck up with neon-pink, yellow and turquoise washi tape.

Seeing beauty in something old and tatty is at the heart of the faded grandeur style. Exposed bare plaster walls, peeling vintage wallpaper, chipped ornate frames and well-worn curtains/drapes may not be everyone's go-to decorating and style choices, but teamed with something grand like an antique crystal chandelier or a glamorously dressed bed, and you have a faded grandeur space full of character.

Faded
GRANDEUR

Faded Grandeur
TEXTURE & TONES

Creating a faded grandeur space or celebrating a worn-out but beautiful room involves a rich mix of textures. The whole style, in fact, is all about discovering rough, interesting and unexpected textures and tones. Architectural details are often enhanced with paint or clever lighting, and rich velvets, sumptuous throws and delicate lace are the go-to textiles. You can buy accessories from antique fairs and junk shops – look for pretty but worn items as well as those 'wow factor' pieces. Most of the textures evolve over time for this look, but there are a few tricks you can try to speed things along, such as leaving textile items in the sun over the summer months to bleach and fade them, experimenting with paint effects on wooden furniture, and creating your own grand floral displays with winter flowers and large antique vases.

When I was growing up, my parents did all the decorating throughout their house themselves, and one of the highlights for me was helping them strip the walls of wallpaper; I loved discovering the layers of old wallpaper and exposing the fabric of the house. Of course, when I was younger, I probably didn't appreciate the beauty of the exposed walls, as I couldn't wait to cover them up with posters of my favourite pop stars. A few years down the line and now the proud owner of a Victorian house, I have been rediscovering the original plaster walls and have left a few exposed. As a tip, instead of spending money on a plasterer to skim your walls perfectly, strip the walls of their current coverings yourself using a wallpaper stripper and stripping knife from your local do-it-yourself store. It will require elbow grease, but it will be worth it to discover what's been hiding underneath!

charming floral displays

A pop of neon-pink ribbon adds a modern edge to this vintage jug/pitcher filled with dried Hydrangeas (top left).
A beautiful vintage corsage in a display bag is stuck to the wall using gold washi tape (top centre). A cut-glass rounded vase of white freesias stands in front of cute, bird-themed collectables (top right). A grand old chair with its exposed springs makes a perfect place for a winter floral display (bottom left). An ornate French picture frame pairs well with this pretty peach lampshade with its faded embroidery floral design and a vase of orange and pink snapdragons (bottom centre). Sumptuous silky cushions/pillows and throws make this bed luxurious and inviting (bottom right).

DRAMATIC LIGHTING

The days are darker and longer in winter, so lighting has never been more welcome. Faded grandeur spaces need to be dramatically and romantically lit, but they don't work well with harsh bright lights. Hunt out unusual candelabras to use as table centrepieces with tapered dinner candles, or buy scented candles in glass jars with interesting labels – I love the scent of Baies by Diptyque. Antique chandeliers and glass pendants will add a sense of drama and elegance to the space. Add dimmer switches to keep the mood intriguing and restful.

flickering candlelight
Painting the ceiling in a dramatic shade and adding flickering candles or nightlights will create pools of light, adding texture to the room and enhancing original mouldings (top left). Look for interesting antique lighting at antique shops, fairs and flea markets. These pretty Italian metal roses and lights (top right) came from Sunbury Antiques Market. Scented candles work well in living rooms and bathrooms. I like musky scents with a nod to the past (bottom left and right). To create a romantic ambience, choose classic church pillar candles (opposite) or scatter tealights along shelves or mantelpieces.

Make a lampshade garland

This gorgeous garland (opposite) makes a unique party or wedding decoration as well as adding some serious style to your boudoir. You will need a collection of small lampshades, a 10-m/30-ft length of stout, coloured twine, three long nails and a hammer. If you can't find enough vintage shades, buy new ones and customize them with fringing or pom-pom trim.

Cut your twine to your desired length, adding a little extra onto each end for tying up the garland later. Thread each lampshade onto the twine and knot it in place, leaving an equal gap between each shade. Hammer the nails into your walls, then tie the twine onto the nails as tightly as possible.

* Style tip

Exposed plaster walls create the most beautiful effect in this bedroom (opposite). If you live in an older property where the walls have been wallpapered, you could discover amazing surfaces beneath it with unique colours, texture and patterns. Make a statement with one bare plaster wall, or for a more dramatic look, peel back the layers around the whole room. For a glamorous effect, dress the bed with jewel-like colours. I added a touch of vibrant pink and layered the bed with vintage eiderdowns in dusky pinks and silky pistachio green in a combination of textiles with embroidered details. These extra layers will most certainly keep you warm and cosy too.

This bedroom has a feminine feel, starting with the lace panel at the window. The bed itself is a regular box-spring divan to which a French whitewashed wooden headboard has been added. I dressed the bed with layers of vintage faded floral eiderdowns with a white crochet floral blanket on top. The cushion/pillow once had a vibrant colourful floral design, but now features soft muted tones after being faded by sunlight. My friend Debbie collects these vintage silk corsages and they work well as a lovely wall display taped in place with gold washi tape.

choosing your colours

There are quite a few options for faded grandeur colour schemes, such as soft pastels and faded floral hues, jewel-like tones with flashes of bright pink, boudoir peach or dark and moody shades. If you are planning to strip your walls and not repaint or paper them, the colours and tones you discover underneath will determine the colour base of the space. If your home boasts period details, such as panelling or an old marble fireplace, you'll need to consider these elements when selecting your colour themes. If you find the perfect shade for your walls on a piece of old ribbon or cloth, take it along to your local do-it-yourself store where they do paint colour matching.

This beautiful box of antique haberdashery is a feast for the eyes, and the colours and tones would create a perfect Faded Grandeur colour scheme (above). A pretty bouquet of pale purple hyacinths sits atop a pile of vintage fabrics.

This hallway (right) and living space (opposite) both boast their original features and their incredible walls reveal their history through the leftover layers of paint. I've added a lace tablecloth to a simple metal folding table and placed a galvanized vase of white Amaryllis on it, which is all the styling this hallway needs as the walls do the talking. The panelled Georgian living room is decorated with a couple of pots of heather, a cosy chair with hand-knitted blankets and a dusky pink cushion/pillow.

A collection of vintage and antique mirrors have been grouped together in this hallway space, where a gorgeous mottled blue wall has been uncovered, leaving remnants of period-style wallpaper (far left). This stack of luxury velvet cushions/pillows will add comfort and style to antique chairs and second-hand sofas. Make your own if you're a whizz on the sewing machine or rummage through textile stalls at flea markets for vintage velvet cushion/pillow covers (left).

understated opulence

The owners of this stunning London apartment have made the most of their spectacular, high-ceilinged eighteenth-century living space by building a mezzanine level. The elegance of the Georgian cornicing works perfectly next to the colour and texture of the bare plaster, while the sconces add extra interest. The low-slung sofa features a mix of dark floral-printed cushions/pillows — I'm always on the hunt for the round style with hand-embroidered centres — silky textures, velvet and neon-pink to keep it on trend. Other ways to add opulence include introducing tassel trims to curtains/drapes and blinds/shades. Liberty of London has a fabulous selection of trims featuring beads and tassels.

I'm love this intricate metal pineapple wall sconce with candleholder from Caravan (right). The owners have created an amazing indoor arbour effect with the antique architectural detailing (overleaf). The mezzanine is the perfect place for a daybed, which adds a sense of decadence to a faded grandeur space.

* *The erosion and evolution that occurs over time is so hard to replicate that it is almost more valuable than new.*

Style tip

Choose an elegant French-style dining table and add interest with antique paintings in ornate frames. I love a touch of gold, and introducing some gilded elements will give your dining room the faded grandeur feel. Look out for antique brass candlesticks at fairs and flea markets, and get creative with some gold leaf to make your own gilded decorative items.

Make a gilt frame

I love using gold leaf for crafting projects and gilding second-hand frames is really easy to do yourself. First you need an old frame, gold-leaf sheets (easy to find online), PVA glue, a glue brush, a dry paintbrush and gold ribbon. Take the backing board and glass away from the frame and discard, then paint the frame lightly with the glue. Next, take the sheets of gold leaf and carefully wrap them around the frame. Smooth it down with the dry brush. Continue until you're happy with the coverage – I like to leave a few gaps to give the frame a textural look. Tie the ribbon around the frame and hang it up, then add a sprig of greenery and a couple of vintage postcards.

Make gilded pear table decorations

For this lovely idea, you need fresh pears with stalks attached, gold-leaf sheets, PVA glue, a glue brush and a dry paintbrush, kraft card tags and a black pen. Paint the pears with the glue and, as delicately as you can, take your gold leaf and apply it using the dry paintbrush. You're aiming for a mottled effect, so don't worry if the gold leaf doesn't completely cover the pear. Leave them to dry and then write your guests' names on the tags with the pen. Once the pears are dry, pop the tag onto the stalk and you're ready to style your table with them.

This pretty café in Halden, Norway, is named Polly's Tearoom, after the English mother of the two sisters who own it. The walls are clad in traditional Scandinavian tongue-and-groove wood and painted white, while the furniture is all sourced from antique and vintage fairs. The interior styling is a mix of Swedish and French, and candles in jars have been placed on every table to welcome customers on this cold November morning. I love the rolls of botanical prints in an old wire basket placed among soup tureens and pots of beautiful white amaryllis.

inspired by the past

Celebrate and be inspired by yesteryear by taking old, worn and threadbare items and giving them a new lease of life in your home.

The best thing about using old, second-hand and antique pieces is that you can pick and choose items from different countries, cultures and eras and create your own unique style. Vintage cafés and restaurants are great places to visit for decorating inspiration, there are more and more unique businesses popping up all over the place at the moment. Visiting a pretty café on a winter's day is a lovely way to while away a few dark and gloomy hours — particularly when it serves yummy hot chocolate/cocoa!

I love styling vignettes on top of cupboards and console tables. Here, I used duck-egg blue tones with an antique birds' egg chart and a pretty Swallow plate by Heart Vintage (below). Snapdragons in a pretty vase are a nice finishing touch. Piles of plates, vintage mirrors and antique salt and pepper shakers make a striking collection (opposite).

When I think about rustic style, the mood I conjure up is earthy, simple and natural. I like to include rustic details that blend really well with country, industrial and retro styles. I'm hugely inspired by old barns, log cabins and even the humble garden shed — wooden structures always have a charming feel — so taking rustic ideas from these shelters will help your home feel like a retreat this winter.

Rustic RETREAT

Rustic Retreat
TEXTURE & TONES

I love nothing better than heading out into the English countryside for a long walk with my family. In autumn, I take colour inspiration from the beautiful changing hues of the leaves, with rich tones of amber, bronze and auburn. When stepping outside in the winter months, though, rustic texture and tones surround us. It's these types of textures that are key to the rustic look and can transform a space. Introducing a natural wood-clad wall into your home will instantly give it a cosy log-cabin feel, while piles of freshly chopped logs, ready to heat up the house, are practical and evoke a feeling of rustic charm.

Rustic winter textiles include cable-knit blankets made from undyed lambswool and a mix of natural linens. Rustic winter tones are earthy and often head towards the dark end of the spectrum. Rich blacks, deep greens and dark wood hues make a good backdrop for natural elements, collections of stoneware and handmade ceramics. Rustic homes are honest and not overstyled – materials such as slate, sheepskin and metals all work well in a rustic space. There are a few different rustic looks which each use slightly different textures and tones: Modern Rustic includes accents of bright colour, Mid-Century Rustic marries retro pieces with earthy tones, and Industrial Rustic celebrates items and materials once used in manufacturing and industrial business, such as work benches and stainless steel.

country life

This winter picnic setting, with hand-knitted gloves and two cups of steaming coffee from the flask, looks inviting with all those cosy blankets and rugs (top left). This extension looks like the perfect rustic cabin – I love the corrugated roof and metal windows (top centre). Honesty's (Lunaria annua) translucent disc-shaped seedpods are a delicate rustic decoration – look out for these on winter walks (top right). How cute are these leaf-design plates by Fine Little Day (available through Pil & Bue) (bottom left)? A pile of logs sits ready to be burned either on a log burner or open fire (bottom centre). I always look out for pretty boxes of matches, as they make great props and add to the style of a lovely fireplace with a roaring fire going (bottom right).

BRING NATURE INDOORS

Bringing a little bit of nature indoors goes a long way during the winter. Splash out on an impressive bouquet of the magical Amaranthus flowers with their trademark cascading tassel flowers or opt for something simple from your own garden – bundles of twigs and branches can add some serious rustic style to your home. Next time you're out on a country walk, look out for pinecones, fallen acorns and horse chestnuts, which look great displayed in glass jars or vases. I also like to use pots of rosemary around my house during winter to add a lovely scent. Of course, many of us bring a living tree into our homes during the Christmas celebrations. I bought a potted tree last year, which I planted in our garden ready to use again this year. For rustic-style decorations you could tie bundles of cinnamon sticks with string and attach them to your tree, and dry out slices of orange to use as ornaments.

✳ *A sprig of something green is sometimes all you need to bring your space to life.*

Simple sprigs cut from a pine or fir tree are a fantastic and easy way to bring nature indoors, as they will last in a vase for ages (opposite left). A vase of showy dark-pink Amaranthus makes an elegant and striking display on this mantelpiece (opposite right). The green pines of this small branch stand out against the dark background and go perfectly with the rustic ceramic urn-style vases. The small concrete plant pots double as candle holders (above left). Beautiful pale-pink snow berries are drying out in the glass jug/pitcher, while a pear sits alongside (above right), forming a simple, impromptu still life.

Make a window decoration

How sweet is this? It's so easy to do – you just
need a collection of dried leaves in a mixture
of colours and shapes. You'll also need a scalpel
knife, cutting mat or thick cardboard and some
washi tape (I used neon pink). Place the leaves
onto the cutting mat or cardboard and use the
scalpel (carefully!) to carve out the letters of
the word you want to spell out. Then, once all
the letters are cut out, tape the leaves to the
window pane to spell out your word.

* *Style tip*

The gorgeous colours of autumn leaves just beg to
be displayed. To create an autumn love heart, pick
up a few fallen leaves on a country walk and arrange
them in a shape of a heart or whatever shape takes
your fancy. I stuck each leaf to the barn door using
neon-pink washi tape. You could also try this idea
above your bed or mantelpiece.

A charming rustic barn makes a perfect venue for a winter wedding or party and can also be used as an extra living space. The key is to retain the charm while making it a useable space. This barn has a power supply, providing lighting and warmth, and some repairs had been done to the roof to prevent leaks and loss of heat. The old horse bridles have been left looped across a beam, which adds to the character and history of the space.

Earthy tones and botanical prints have been mixed with a retro easy chair in this Norwegian living space (left). The different textiles create interest and comfort, and the corner sofa offers an inviting space for all the family. Collections of artwork, photography and prints have been grouped together on the walls and the vintage floral cushions/pillows in browns and orange tones give the modern sofas a retro feel (opposite).

mid-century rustic

This style blends a retro style of furniture with rustic colours and wood-clad walls, as you can see in this traditional wooden house set in the Norwegian countryside, decorated with vintage and rustic finds mixed with modern essentials and rustic styling. Mid-Century Modern describes a design period from roughly 1933–65, when designers such as Charles and Ray Eames and British furniture manufacturer Ercol were designing high-quality pieces of modern furniture with clean lines. I love how the classic designs are still very on-trend 40 years on. I like to mix rustic elements with classic 1960s designs to create an eclectic rustic style.

rustic living

This huge, rustic wood kitchen table is where the family hangs out. There is a mix of Mid-Century Eames chairs, industrial-style work chairs and second-hand wooden chairs. The rustic natural-wood wall stands next to the collection of framed prints and artworks, which have been grouped together alongside a bold wall calendar. The retro-style brass half-globe pendant light is the perfect height for overhead soft lighting, while the handmade copper-pipe candelabra adds a cool industrial touch (opposite). The Fine Little Day autumn-leaves ceramics are well-suited to this room. It's a cosy space for a lovely cup of tea (above). This old rustic wood ladder, leaning against a natural wood-clad wall, makes a great place to hang blankets (above right). Framed by the amazing wooden wall, the white living space features a Mid-Century Modern shelving unit that houses the family's books (below right).

dark & handsome

As much as I love light and airy spaces, there's a place in my heart for the dark and handsome, too. Dark wood has been out of favour for the last few years, with many people, including me, painting wooden furniture white or opting for lighter woods. But now that dark wood is making a return, why not make the most of by teaming dark architectural furniture and ceramics with a dark painted wall to create a striking combination. A moodier colour palette can add depth, tone and drama to a rustic space. Experiment with handsome shades of dark inky blues, darker shades of grey and dirty olive greens. Panelled walls definitely benefit from a dark covering, as the details tend to stand out.

Inside this Danish cabin a large pine in a galvanized bucket makes quite a statement on the table (above left). The retro-style round table and industrial-style wooden and metal chairs make an eclectic combination. The wooden veranda wall (opposite) has been painted in Valspar's Dark Kettle Black – the large rustic table looks great against this handsome shade.

soft, moody tones

This beautiful velvet armchair with its comfortable faux-fur rug provides a snug place next to the fireplace to sit, read, craft and sip hot chocolate/cocoa (opposite). It sits perfectly in front of the soft, moody tones of the panelled walls. Black tiles, worktops and a black aga are teamed with this lovely Secret Moss colour by Valspar, which has been painted on the walls and cupboards (below). It's certainly dramatic but also feels cosy (this page).

Make a rustic garland

You'll need a collection of papers in your choice of colours (here I used a mix of patterned and plain brown papers), scissors, a pencil, leaves to act as templates and pictures of woodland animals for copying or tracing. You'll also need a sewing machine that can cope with sewing through paper and thread of your choice. Place the leaves on the paper and draw around them, then draw or trace some woodland animals (I've gone for rabbits and squirrels). Cut out all the shapes and sew them together, pulling the thread to leave a gap between each character, but not cutting it. Make the garland to your desired length and then cut off the thread and tape the top of the thread to the wall.

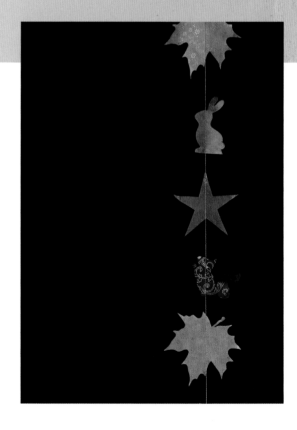

Make a pinecone wall display

To make this pine cone wall decoration, you'll need a collection of pinecones, natural string, scissors and an old branch from a tree. Simply tie each pinecone stalk onto a length of string and then knot the other end to the wood or branch. Repeat with all the pinecones, tying them at different lengths to make a pattern. Then take another length of string and tie it onto the wood to make a loop for hanging. Finally, find a good space in your rustic home to hang your new wall decoration.

the scout hut

Built in the 1900s, this former scout hut is now a holiday/vacation retreat, converted by Vintage Vacations. It's situated in an area of outstanding beauty on the Isle of Wight, UK. Holiday/vacation retreats can often inspire ideas for decorating and styling our homes, as can some older community buildings. In this charming space, the main entrance to the hall features the original Victorian wooden doors and panelling. On the table sits a pretty vintage flask, used as a vase for red berries, and a mini Christmas tree, which looks cute with its pot wrapped in vintage floral fabric. A mezzanine floor was built into the vast space to make the most of the high celling, and now the living area features the pitch of the roof, making the space feel like an attic.

A pair of retro chairs have been positioned under the wooden eaves on the new mezzanine level facing the window (below left). During its refurbishment, the new owners created a wooden balcony and deck, where their guests can enjoy the stunning views – the perfect place to enjoy a hot drink wrapped in a blanket (below).

During the winter months the weather offers us a range of white delights to inspire us, such as delicate snowflakes, morning frost and pale skies. A blanket of newly fallen snow is a magical sight and makes everything look clean and fresh. I love to bring some of the joy of snow into interior styling. White is possibly my favourite colour to decorate with – it's classic, calm, clean and never goes out of fashion.

Winter
WHITES

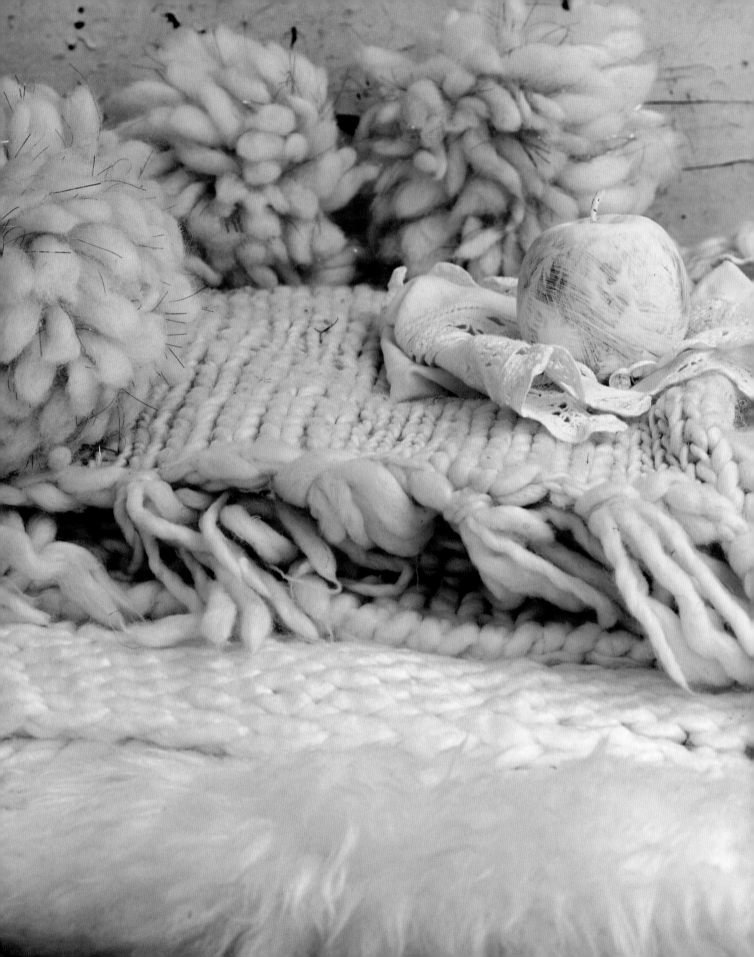

Winter whites
TEXTURE & TONES

White, in all its many shades – from cool pale greys to warm, buttery creams – always creates tranquil rooms, and using a rich mix of textures will prevent it from looking bland. A pale, bleached hue is a versatile base for a number of different looks, and there are so many variations in the white palette that you can always achieve fresh, new effects. Inspired by some of the homes I have visited in Scandinavian countries, where it's common to use lots of white in the home to maximize light during the dark winters, I have become a huge fan of white-painted wooden floors, which make a great backdrop to almost any style of furniture. I love how the natural texture and grain of the wood can still be seen, but the overall look and feel is light and bright.

Adding different textures to our homes is something many of us do naturally every six months or so, or whenever the seasons change. As the temperatures start to drop, introduce some warm, chunky knitted or crocheted blankets and throws to beds, sofas and chairs. Bare floors benefit from a scattering of winter rugs; and light and breezy voile curtains can be swapped for thicker or lined window treatments that keep out chilly winter draughts. With all-white spaces, it's the tones and textures that add detail and interest, so think about adding different items – shaggy sheepskins, linen cushions/pillows, painted wood – in varying shades of white; and to keep your space feeling cosy head towards the warmer tones in the white palette.

pale and interesting

I love these knitted blankets in ivory and the palest grey. Thrown over the arm of a sofa, they always look effortlessly chic and cosy (top left). I bought this vintage wire basket for my white-painted living room from a flea market, and I love filling it with freshly chopped logs (top centre). The paper origami hanging decoration adds a pretty handmade charm and another texture to the space (top right). White Amaryllis flowers look stunning in these clear glass jars (bottom left). A collection of tealights in glass jars creates a pretty display in this vintage cake tin/pan (bottom centre). There's nothing like the warmth of a thick winter rug to add style and texture to a room (bottom right).

MAGICAL LIGHTING

In the winter months, without the natural light streaming through the windows as much as it does in summer, getting the lighting in your home right is crucial. Winter's the perfect time to put up a set of fairy/string lights to give your space a magical feel and, of course candles have their place too. Other lighting ideas include industrial-chic bare lightbulbs, which have in recent years been used as a feature. A collection of different soft lighting ideas works together to make a space feel cosy. So, experiment with a mix of table lamps, festoon lights and filament bulbs.

feature lighting ideas
Church pillar candles in glass jars light the way up this wide set of white-painted stairs (top left).
I love this idea of taking a string of festoon lights and folding the cable together to create a bundle of pendant lights, held together by black cable ties (top right). Look out for interesting lightbulbs in specialist lighting stores, such as filament bulbs, metallic dips that bounce the light upwards, and unusual shapes like teardrops and goblets (bottom left). This string of lights featuring white origami lanterns are a pretty detail simply hung from a hook in this hallway (bottom right).

Make fairy/string light bunting

Bunting doesn't have to just be something for the warmer months. Here's a wonderfully simple, cheap and pretty idea to fill an indoor space with a sense of celebration. I love using fairy/string lights in my home and I keep them up all year round – the light is so soft and pretty that it gives any space some ambience. Here, I first suspended a set of string lights across the room. To make the bunting, I hung up some string above and below the lights and then cut out long rectangular pieces of lace paper and parcel paper, which I folded tightly over the string at regular intervals. You can secure the paper with a little piece of sticky tape on the inside of the fold if you need to.

Make a moss candle arrangement

For this earthy lighting display, you need some dinner candles, moss and a large dish or bowl. I collected this moss while out on a winter walk and later arranged it in a large wooden dish. Sink the candles into the moss so that they are secure and stand upright. This idea could also work for individual candles placed in moss-filled plant pots or jars. Let the candles burn down but keep an eye on them once they get close to the moss and replace them with new candles. This is a good idea for a table centrepiece for winter celebrations.

romantic whites

When creating a romantic interior, faded winter whites work perfectly. The key design elements of the scheme shown on these pages are vintage and French-inspired. Salvaged and antique pieces are arranged in a pared-down space with a delicate, feminine atmosphere. To re-create this effect, walls can either be papered with a pretty, pale design or painted in gentle off-whites. Leave wood floors bare or paint or bleach them white. Furniture is a mix of vintage upholstered, wood and metal, shapely and elegant in form. As with most interior schemes, it's the details that tie the look together. Here, decorative touches include a pair of vintage skates hung from a door handle and vintage metal tartlet tins used as dainty tealight holders.

In this Norwegian home, the wood-clad walls and celling have all been painted white. The wooden country table (above left) is unpainted, whereas the dining table has had its base painted creamy white (opposite). Instead of flowers, bare twigs and pinecone-studded branches make a dramatic seasonal decoration (above and opposite).

catching the light

A collection of mercury glass and vintage baubles makes a striking display along a mantelpiece. The silver tones in the glass vases reflect the white-painted walls and the pinecones add to the wintery feel (opposite). White-painted wood cladding has been used to decorate the walls of this Norwegian home (this page). A Victorian garden urn has been brought indoors to become a fancy pot for a house plant. The white goose adds a touch of elegance to the scene.

Make pinecone firelighters

To make these pretty firelighters, you will need tealights (at least 2 cm/¾ in. deep), pinecones, an oven, cupcake cases and a baking sheet lined with greaseproof paper. First, preheat the oven to 170°C (325°F) Gas 3. Remove the metal case from each tealight and then arrange the cupcake cases on the baking sheet. Place a tealight into each of the cases, keeping the wicks in place, and put them in the preheated oven for 5 minutes, or until the wax has melted. Remove the baking sheet from the oven and carefully position the wick to the edge of the case. Place a pinecone inside each case and leave at room temperature for the wax to set. Once they have set, remove the cases and your firelighters are ready.

* *Style tip*

If you're looking for a simple decoration for your white interior scheme, then how about painting some apples with white emulsion/latex paint for a new idea? Once the paint is dry, arrange the apples in a row on a shelf or sideboard. I roughly painted these Granny Smith apples as I liked the mottled finish. This technique also works with other fruits, particularly pears. You could also use them to decorate place settings if you're throwing a festive celebration or dinner party (see page 81).

home-made delights

The corner of this pretty Norwegian café has been styled ready for the festive season – the pot of this real Christmas tree has been wrapped in French hessian cloth and the tree has been adorned with a few vintage decorations and a giant star on top. I love the mix of different textures and tones of white in the space. The bench sofa is a warm ivory colour, while the cotton cushions/pillows are pure white. The old French window panel painted in greyish white now frames a metal candelabra. Candles in glass jars have been placed in a large vintage cake tin/pan on this sweet little table. It's a very inviting space.

A collection of glass bottles and dried hydrangea
flowers makes a pretty display on this window ledge.
Collect glass bottles in different sizes and shapes to
make a similar arrangement and use a mix of dried
hydrangeas, thistles, poppy seed heads and teasels.
For a white scheme choose clear glass or glass with
a soft hue of dusky pink or amber.

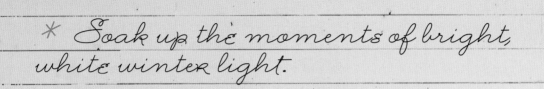

* Soak up the moments of bright, white winter light.

northern light

The Scandinavian countries are well known for their beautiful light, even though the hours of daylight are few and far between during the winter. Artists make the most of the light with studios set up near windows and their work spaces are often painted in shades of white to reflect even more light back into the area. When there is a blanket of snow outside and a few rays of sun filter inside, the rooms appear brilliant white. Once the evening draws in or on grey days, artificial lighting is used to replicate natural light. Anglepoise lamps work well for task lighting and clear filament bulbs with brass fittings offer both an attractive light and a touch of industrial chic.

A narrow console table – constructed from an old piece of wood and white metal table legs from IKEA – makes a good place to display collections. The white-painted wood walls bounce the light around the room and offer a simple backdrop for the artworks (opposite). This work space has been set up directly under the window to make the most of the natural light. The piece of pretty lace fabric diffuses the light nicely (below right). The easel and palettes introduce colour to this mostly white space (below left).

flexible friends

This white Norwegian studio is equipped with a modern kitchen, and this quirky trolley table offers an extra worktop as well as storage (left). In the centre of the studio is a harmonious seating area with a white two-seater sofa, and a rustic coffee table made from an old piece of wood on castors. On the table is a tray of white porcelain vases and candles. The original Ercol spindle-back chairs are painted in two shades of delicate salmon pink (below). An old industrial plan chest is a great place to store books and papers. The posters have been tacked to the wall unframed, and a green wreath bound in white pom-pom trim dangles from the ceiling (opposite).

✳ Style tip

Here, the letter 'F' stands for 'fryd' in Norwegian, which translates as 'joy'. To make this bold wall letter, an outline of pins have been carefully pushed into the wooden wall so that black wool can be wound tightly around them. The bottom of the letter has been decorated with hanging bells and tassels, which were simply knotted on. You could use this idea on the door to your children's rooms, although it will be much more difficult with a curved letter like 'S' for Selina!

Make garland decorations

For this bell garland (below), you'll just need a length of string and some bells (the type with little ridges or hooks). Put a bell on the string and twist the wire by turning the bell around once. Repeat at regular intervals, twisting the wire to attach each bell until you get to the end of your wire. To make a tissue-paper flower garland (right), layer 8–10 sheets of tissue paper and fold them concertina-style. Secure the folds in the centre with string and snip the ends of the folded paper to form semicircular shapes. Then open out the papers to make a fan shape and start lifting each individual layer of tissue paper. Make a few and tie them onto a length of string.

It's the most wonderful time of the year … the weather outside might be frightful, but winter is most definitely party season. With many celebrations in autumn and winter, it's certainly time for some home-made decorations, party styling and super-stylish table settings. Whether you love traditional decorations, prefer a pop of modern colour or like to keep things natural, this chapter will fill you with ideas for styling your own celebrations.

Festive
CELEBRATIONS

MAKING AN ENTRANCE

Hanging foliage wreaths on the front door is a tradition I love to do in the run-up to Christmas. Typically, wreaths were made from evergreens, which symbolize strength, but they can also be made from an assortment of flowers, leaves, fruits and twigs constructed in a ring shape. I like making wreaths in every season: Easter wreaths in pastel colours with spring flowers, fragrant rose wreaths for summer parties, autumn wreaths celebrating the rich tones and, of course, Christmas wreaths for welcoming guests to your home. Another option for dressing doors is to suspend a foliage garland above and around the top of the door frame. If you're keen to try something different this year you could bundle together a simple posy of pine sprigs and tie it with a ribbon bow, then hang it upside down from the door knocker.

Making a wreath for my front door marks the beginning of the Christmas festivities.

door dress-up

Autumn wreaths are a great way to bring the seasonal tones into your home, and are perfect for Halloween and harvest festivals (opposite left). A natural pine wreath tied with a simple sage-coloured satin ribbon bow looks striking against this copper backdrop (opposite right). This Danish cabin door is dressed with a garland and sprigs of pine tied with neon-pink ribbon (above).

I'm a huge fan of waxflowers – I wore them in my hair on my Wedding day. For this pretty wreath, I cut small sprigs of the flowers and stuck them, along with pine sprigs, into a soaked oasis wreath. I added a length of dusky-pink ribbon tied in a bow (above right). This berry wreath, adorning a sky-blue door, was made from items found in the garden and a little wire to secure the berry sprigs in place (right).

How cute are these embroidered napkins from Anthropologie? They're perfect for serving guests mince pies and nibbles (left). Most of my vintage baubles are from charity shops, but I also found a few at a flea market just outside Paris (right). I made this wreath of gold leaves with 1950s leaf decorations that I bought at a flea market – each leaf has a wire stalk that I wrapped around a metal wreath frame (below).

vintage christmas

I've been collecting vintage glass tree ornaments and baubles for years. Some have been passed down to me through my family and others I've bought in second-hand shops/thrift stores and at antiques fairs. I'm drawn to the pretty jewel colours and hand-painted details. The scent of a real tree reminds me of childhood Christmases, and I love the tree's natural shape. This year I chose a potted spruce that I could plant in our garden. For winter I put down this gorgeous vintage-style Moroccan Benni rug from The Plantation Rug Company, which is so cosy underfoot. A real fire is a joy and instantly creates warmth and atmosphere. I love styling my marble mantelpiece with frames, candles, orange pomanders and leftover baubles.

country christmas

An Inglenook fireplace, real tree and roaring fire set the scene for a cosy Christmas in this English country cottage. Decorating ideas are simple and beautiful, and blend creative home-made decorations with rustic items/pieces and a touch of vintage. The Country Christmas style is all about getting crafty, home baking and being creative with what nature has to offer. Whether you live in a rural setting or a city dwelling, you can create a Country look with my decorating ideas, a couple of pots of heather and a few vintage elements.

Traditional red and green colours have been replaced with raspberry, bright pink, purple and olive green to decorate this tree. Homespun decorations are mixed with vintage and new ones to add warmth and character. This space invites you to take a seat and put your feet up by the fire (right).

pretty paper chains
For me, the festive period is
a time to get crafting. I make
my own cards, gift tags and
decorations, including classic
paper chains, which I loved
making as a child and still do.
Here, I used a mix of papers
printed with classic designs
from Liberty of London.

Make felt bunting

To make this lovely festive decoration (below), you need red and green felt (I used a mix of light and dark green with raspberry red), red cotton thread, fabric scissors and a sewing machine (although you could sew it by hand if you have plenty of time). First, cut out a selection of holly shapes in both shades of green felt – you could do this by eye or make a template if you're not that confident. Next, cut circles from the red felt to make the berries. Thread up your sewing machine with the red cotton thread and start sewing the shapes together – one leaf followed by a holly berry – by sewing down the centre of each shape using a straight stitch. Continue until you're happy with the length.

Make patchwork tree baubles

This is a great way to give old baubles a new lease of life. You'll need plastic baubles, fabric, PVA glue and a glue brush, fabric scissors and a narrow ribbon. Cut your chosen fabrics into small squares or rectangles pieces – they don't all have to be the same size, so don't worry about being too neat. Once you have a pile of fabric pieces ready, use a paint brush to cover the bauble with PVA glue, then start sticking them on, overlapping the pieces so there aren't any gaps. Make a loop from the ribbon and hang it up to dry.

natural christmas

Christmas doesn't have to be all about the glitz and glamour – you can create beautiful Christmas decor with natural materials. Undyed hessian works well as a tablecloth alongside linen napkins, and kraft card is ideal for making your own name-place cards. When you're styling your natural Christmas dining table, try and mix up different natural materials to create interest and style. I like to use slate tiles as place mats, natural linen napkins and recycled glass jars for tealight holders. A couple of terracotta pots of rosemary make a great centrepiece. Mini potted pine trees can be simply dressed with white twinkly fairy/string lights, and tealights in a mix of glass jars are essential for creating a soft ambience.

Why not draw directly onto a window using a non-permanent glass pen? Here I've used a white pen to draw 'Let it snow' on the pane with little dots to represent snow – kids love it (above left). I've mixed tealight holders of all shapes and sizes, from a simple jam/jelly jar to a rounded vase and a more intricate cut-glass option (above). Simple brown parcel paper is perfect for wrapping gifts, tied up with string or ribbon and decorated with pine sprigs (opposite top left). How sweet is this cutlery/flatware set with the kraft name place tied with twine and garnished with greenery (opposite below).

Make christmas tags & cards

Scan your artwork or use an image you have saved
to your computer. Open a photo-editing program,
such as Photoshop, or an online photo-editing website
and make a grid of images to cover an A4/US letter size
area. I managed to fit eight images onto my sheet so
each tag is 7.5 x 10.5 cm/3 x 4 inches. Adjust the colour
and tone if desired – I took out some saturation to
make my tree image more tonal. When you're happy,
print it onto white card and cut them out. Then cut
kraft parcel tags into strips, add a Christmas label
and tie them all together with sliver thread or string.
Finally, fix them onto your wrapped gifts.

After decorating my Christmas tree, I used leftover vintage baubles as a table display arranged in a glass dish (far left). I made this lovely wreath candle decoration (left) by fashioning two circlular shapes with rustic string wire and then attaching fir sprigs to them using craft wire. I then secured twigs to the bottom wreath to support the top wreath. Next, I inserted candleholders around the top wreath and added long candles. The stunning naked cake takes pride of place surrounded by festive cookies, the vintage baubles and the wreath candle decoration (below).

traditional christmas

A characterful old wooden table surrounded by a mix of different style chairs is how I like dining spaces to look. Adding a beautiful floral arrangement is almost all you need to create a magical Christmas setting. Dark wood furniture has slightly fallen out of favour in the past few years with the fashion for white-washing and using clever paint effects to hide and revamp old-fashioned furniture. Now that our love of dark wooden pieces is returning, I like finding old chairs in charity shops and celebrating the areas damaged over time and the slightly faded or worn seats. Mixing these dark-stained antiques with simple white candles and classic florals is a sure-fire way to create a traditional look at Christmas.

Make mulled cider

To make this delightfully festive, warming treat, you will need: 2 litres/quarts of good-quality cider, 6 cloves, 3–4 star anise, a pinch of nutmeg, 1 cinnamon stick, freshly squeezed juice of 1 orange, 1 litre/quart of fresh apple juice and 1 sliced apple. First, pour the cider and apple juice into a large saucepan over a low heat and let it warm through for a few minutes. Add the spices and freshly squeezed orange juice and bring the mixture to the boil, then turn it down and simmer for 5 minutes. Turn the mixture off and pour it into a suitable drinks dispenser or a punch bowl and add the sliced apples for extra flavour and decoration. Serve while it's still warm!

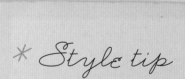

* *Style tip*

To decorate your dining space, use vintage plates (left), jugs/pitchers filled with flowers (opposite) and a few extra sprigs of foliage and red berries to jolly up every dark corner. A classic tapered dinner candle placed in a suitable holder will give the table some elegance, and a drinks dispenser (above) will impress your guests and allows them to help themselves, which frees up the host. Look out for old dark wood furniture in second-hand shops/thrift stores – you'll be amazed at how cheaply you could pick up a beautiful traditional piece.

Fruits are a cheap way to bring a colour to your place settings and these satsumas look great placed in the centre of each plate. I also like to use pomegranates, figs and pears to add colour and interest. Head to your local fruit and vegetable market to buy extra fruits to be used as decorations. I like to save the satsumas that I find in the bottom of my Christmas stocking and put them to good use. You could also try making frosted fruit decorations – made by brushing the fruit with a thin layer of egg white and then coating it with sugar before leaving it to dry. Make sure you don't leave them to dry on paper towels, though, as they will stick to it!

colour-pop party

Adding in bright accents of colour to a party table will jazz up any space and get it party-ready. Often you may need to push a couple of tables together to make room for all your guests, so instead of covering the whole thing in a tablecloth, why not make a feature of the different surfaces. Add colour interest with the candles – here I used my favourite neon-pink dinner candles from True Grace, which stand out against the grey backdrop. Pink Honeycomb pom-poms from Talking Tables add to the fesive mood and details like the red stripey straws and bold floral arrangements take the party from fun to fab.

I love stringing up my festoon lights, which I bought to decorate my wedding venue a few years ago. I use them for loads of occasions as they can be used both inside and out. This cosy cabin definitely benefits from a little overhead light (above).

new year's eve

A rustic barn is a perfect place to host a New Year's Eve party if you're lucky enough to have access to one. I styled this New Year's Eve dinner table with white and green and added metallic elements along with plenty of faux furs, snug blankets and a few plug-in heaters to keep guests warm. Down the middle of the table I scattered fresh green pickings from the garden to create a centrepiece and then I arranged pots of hyacinths, hellebores with candles and oversized gold baubles. The cute mini bundt cakes made by Retro Sugar have been piled onto two-cake stands balanced on top of each other, and the sparklers add the New Year vibe. Above the table hangs a giant honeycomb bauble decoration from Talking Tables.

easy festive decorations
Tie cutlery/flatware sets together with gold tinsel string to add sparkle to each place setting (top left).
Get creative with mini canvases and photocopied Christmassy images to create your own canvases
to decorate your venue (top right). This pretty Christmas wreath has been revamped in time for
the New Year's Eve celebrations with some fresh white roses and ivy from the garden (bottom left).
Can't find any plant pots to match your theme? Wrap them with fabric and tie them up with string
for an instant fix (bottom right).

Sources

Selina Lake
Stylist & author
www.selinalake.co.uk
www.selinalake.blogspot.
com
@selinalake

Libby Summers
www.libbysummers.co.uk
Hand-knitted accessories
for you and your home
including cosy knit socks,
plus knitting patterns,
yarns and knitting kits and
accessories.

Cox and Cox
www.coxandcox.co.uk
Homeware and home
accessories including cosy
cushions, hygge throws and
scented candles.

H&M Home
www.hm.com
Stylish rugs, throws,
blankets and bedding
perfect for Winter Living.

**The Plantation Rug
Company**
www.plantationrug.co.uk
A large collection of rugs to
suit all styles, I love their
Benni range of Moroccan
Style rugs.

Heals
www.heals.co.uk
Modern, designer and
contemporary furniture and
home accessories.

Plum & Ashby
www.plumandashby.co.uk
Spun and woven
accessories for the home
and amazing home and
body products – I love
their Rosemary and Plum
hand wash and Honey and
Amber scented candle.

Honest
www.honestskincare.co.uk
Online vendor of organic
handmade skincare and
candles. I love their pine-
scented candle – perfect
for Winter Living homes.

Paper collective
www.papercollective.com
Iconic and unique design
posters and prints by top
graphic designers, artists
and illustrators.

Fine Little Day
www.finelittleday.com
Lovely homeware designed
in Sweden.

Linwood Fabrics
www.linwoodfabric.com
Great collection of fabric
and wallpaper.

ACR Stoves
acrheatproducts.com
A range of wood burning
stoves to suit all spaces. I
love our Malvern ACR stove
installed in our dining room.

Toast
www.toa.st
Simple and inspiring clothes
and home accessories for
modern living.

The People Shop
50 Poplar Road
Kings Heath
Birmingham
B14 7AG
+44 (0)121 444 3444
www.thepeopleshop.co.uk
A colourful and friendly
shop run by a husband and
wife duo. They sell clothes
and handmade accessories
including neon pink pom-
pom tea cosies.

Diptyque
www.diptyqueparis.co.uk
Scented candles and room
fragrances. I especially love
the Baies scent.

True Grace
www.truegrace.co.uk
Online vendor of scented
candles, diffusers and
home fragrances. I love
their neon-pink dinner
candles and their classic
Moroccan rose-scented
natural wax candle.

Mabel & Bird
mabelandbird.bigcartel.com
Small textile studio in
Oxfordshire producing
handmade screen-
printed homewares and
accessories. I love their
cushions, garlands and
linen pouches.

The Linen Works
www.thelinenworks.co.uk
Pure linen products
including bedlinen,
tablecloths, napkins
and more.

**Grandiflora Home &
Garden**
719 Grover Street,
Lynden, WA
USA 98264
+1 360 318 8854
www.grandiflorahome.com
Lovely shop selling vintage
pieces and vintage-inspired
items for home and garden.

Decopompoms
www.decopompoms.co.uk
Tissue paper pom-poms, honeycomb pom-poms, pretty garlands and lots more party props and decorations.

Talking Tables
www.talkingtables.co.uk
International supplier of fun and stylish party accessories.

Ginger Ray
www.gingerray.co.uk
Unique party and event props and decorations.

Liberty
Regent Street
London
W1B 5AH
www.liberty.co.uk
One of London's oldest department stores selling innovative and eclectic designs. Also features a wonderful haberdashery department.

Caravan
www.caravanstyle.com
Online store run by Emily Chambers, featuring a mix of vintage and unique finds for your home.

IKEA
www.ikea.com
Affordable modern furnishings for the home and garden, with stores worldwide.

Ercol
www.ercol.com
Quality handmade furniture company started in 1920. Buy new pieces direct or look out for their vintage pieces of furniture at flea markets and antique shops.

Sunbury Antiques Market
Kempton Park Racecourse
Staines Road East,
Sunbury on Thames
Middlesex TW16 5AQ
www.sunburyantiques.com
My nearest antiques market, which is held on the second and last Tuesday of each month. A great place to search out vintage lighting, Mid-century Modern pieces and floral fabrics. Well worth a visit!

Folly & Glee
www.follyandglee.co.uk
Preloved and homemade items, including crochet hangers and bakers' twine.

Anthropologie
www.anthropologie.com
Unique cermets and glassware with products sourced around the world. Stores across the USA and Europe including a great store in my home town of Guildford.

Deborah Bowness
www.deborahbowness.com
Beautiful and unusual wallpapers and panels including Christmas tree prints and vintage florals.

Etsy
www.etsy.com
Online worldwide marketplace for small businesses and craftspeople selling homemade and vintage items for home and garden.

Folksy
www.folksy.com
UK-based online store selling homemade items for home and garden.

Hobbycraft
www.hobbycraft.co.uk
Arts and crafts superstores throughout the UK.

PAINTS

Farrow & Ball
www.farrow-ball.com
Great collection of paints and wall coverings. I recommend their Great White floor primer and floor paint for perfect Scandi-inspired wooden floors.

Plastikote
www.plasti-kote.com
A selection of spray paints, which can be used to transform second-hand furniture pieces, metal trays and bedsteads.

Dulux
www.dulux.com

Valpsar
www.valsparpaint.com

BUYING SECOND-HAND
Search for local charity shops/thrift stores, flea markets, vintage fairs, junk shops, yard sales, antique events, car boot sales and auctions rooms.

Picture credits

Endpapers styled by Selina Lake at her home; 1 Jonathan Birch/ Narratives; 2 Gary Yeowell/Mainstream; 3–5 Jeanette Lunde www.madeofrocks.com; 6 left Stella Willing stylist/designer and owner of the house/Ph. Debi Treloar; 6 right – 7 The family home of designer and shop owner An-Magritt Moen in Norway; 9 Stylist Atlanta Bartlett/Ph. Polly Wreford; 10 Pavel Vakhrushev/ Shutterstock; 10 right Styled by Selina Lake at her home; 11 left and centre Styled by Selina Lake at her home; 11 right Lykkeoglykkeliten.blogspot.com/Ph. Debi Treloar; 12 left Styled by Selina Lake at her home; 12 right Jonathan Birch/Narratives; 13 left The home of Yvonne Eijkenduijn of Yvestown.com in Belgium/Ph. Catherine Gratwicke; 13 centre Debi Treloar's home available to hire for shoots www.debitreloar.com; 14 centre Styled by Selina Lake at her home; 14 right Debi Treloar's home available to hire for shoots www.debitreloar.com; 15 The home of the designer Stine and Henrik Busk; 16–17 Sven Hagolani/Getty Images; 18 The home of the designer Stine and Henrik Busk; 19 The Mission and The Scout Hall are available for holiday hire at www.vintagevacations.co.uk; 20–21 Styled by Selina Lake at her home; 22 Debi Treloar's home available to hire for shoots www.debitreloar.com; 23 Styled by Selina Lake at her home; 24 centre Jeanette Lunde www.madeofrocks.com; 24 right The family home of designer and shop owner An-Magritt Moen in Norway; 24 below Styled by Selina Lake at her home; 26 and 27 above right Styling assistance by Debbie Johnson of Powder Blue – Styling Props Locations www.powder-blue.co.uk; 27 above left The Mission and The Scout Hall are available for holiday hire at www.vintagevacations.co.uk; 28 left and 29 right The Mission and The Scout Hall are available for holiday hire at www.vintagevacations.co.uk; 29 left Debi Treloar's home available to hire for shoots www.debitreloar.com; 30 right and 31 Styled by Selina Lake at her home; 34 The family home of designer and shop owner An-Magritt Moen in Norway; 35 The home of the designer Stine and Henrik Busk; 37 above left Styled by Selina Lake at her home; 37 above right The home of the designer Stine and Henrik Busk; 37 below left The Mission and The Scout Hall are available for holiday hire at www.vintagevacations.co.uk; 37 below right Styling assistance by Debbie Johnson of Powder Blue – Styling Props Locations www.powder-blue.co.uk; 38–39 Debi Treloar's home available to hire for shoots www.debitreloar. com; 42 Polly's Tearoom, Halden, Norway; 43 above left, above centre, below left and below centre Debi Treloar's home available to hire for shoots www.debitreloar.com; 43 below right Styled by Selina Lake at her home; 44 The Mission and The Scout Hall are available for holiday hire at www.vintagevacations.co.uk; 48 right Polly's Tearoom, Halden, Norway; 52 right Styling assistance by Debbie Johnson of Powder Blue – Styling Props Locations www. powder-blue.co.uk; 54–55 The family home of designer and shop owner An-Magritt Moen in Norway; 56–57 The Mission and The Scout Hall are available for holiday hire at www.vintagevacations. co.uk; 60 left The Mission and The Scout Hall are available for holiday hire at www.vintagevacations.co.uk; 60 right Debi Treloar's

home available to hire for shoots www.debitreloar.com; 62–63 Styling assistance by Debbie Johnson of Powder Blue – Styling Props Locations www.powder-blue.co.uk; 66 Debi Treloar's home available to hire for shoots www.debitreloar.com; 67 above centre, above right and below Styling assistance by Debbie Johnson of Powder Blue – Styling Props Locations www.powder-blue.co.uk; 68 above and 69 Styling assistance by Debbie Johnson of Powder Blue – Styling Props Locations www.powder-blue.co.uk; 68 below left The home of the designer Stine and Henrik Busk; 70–74 Styling assistance by Debbie Johnson of Powder Blue – Styling Props Locations www.powder-blue.co.uk; 76 above left and below Debi Treloar's home available to hire for shoots www.debitreloar.com; 82–83 Polly's Tearoom, Halden, Norway; 84 Styling assistance by Debbie Johnson of Powder Blue – Styling Props Locations www.powder-blue.co.uk; 85 Polly's Tearoom, Halden, Norway; 90 below centre and right The home of the designer Stine and Henrik Busk; 92 left The family home of designer and shop owner An-Magritt Moen in Norway; 92 right Styling assistance by Debbie Johnson of Powder Blue – Styling Props Locations www.powder-blue.co.uk; 93 left The home of the designer Stine and Henrik Busk; 93 right Styling assistance by Debbie Johnson of Powder Blue – Styling Props Locations www.powder-blue.co.uk; 94 The Mission and The Scout Hall are available for holiday hire at www.vintagevacations.co.uk; 98–101 The family home of designer and shop owner An-Magritt Moen in Norway; 102–103 The home of the designer Stine and Henrik Busk; 104–105 Styling assistance by Debbie Johnson of Powder Blue – Styling Props Locations www.powder-blue.co.uk; 106 left The family home of designer and shop owner An-Magritt Moen in Norway; 106 right–107 The home of the designer Stine and Henrik Busk; 108–109 The Mission and The Scout Hall are available for holiday hire at www.vintagevacations.co.uk; 110–111 Hanne Gran's home, Halden, Norway; 114 Styled by Selina Lake at her home; 115 above left, above centre and below right Styled by Selina Lake at her home; 115 above right and below left Jeanette Lunde www.madeofrocks.com; 115 below centre Polly's Tearoom, Halden, Norway; 116 above left Styled by Selina Lake at her home; 116 above right and below Jeanette Lunde www.madeofrocks.com; 118–119 Jeanette Lunde www.madeofrocks.com; 120–123 Hanne Gran's home, Halden, Norway; 124 Styled by Selina Lake at her home; 125 Polly's Tearoom, Halden, Norway; 126–133 Jeanette Lunde www.madeofrocks.com; 135 Fabulous Vintage Finds www. fabulousvintagefinds.com; 136 left The Mission and The Scout Hall are available for holiday hire at www.vintagevacations.co.uk; 136 right Debi Treloar's home available to hire for shoots www. debitreloar.com; 137 above left The home of the designer Stine and Henrik Busk; 137 above right and 138 Styled by Selina Lake at her home; 139 above left Debi Treloar's home available to hire for shoots www.debitreloar.com; 139 above right and below Styled by Selina Lake at her home; 140 Håkan Jansson/Folio; 144 and 145 above Styled by Selina Lake at her home; 160 Styled by Selina Lake at her home.

Business credits

Helen Bratby
Barn and farmhouse
available for location hire
near Cranbrook in Kent.
Contact Helen Bratby on
+44 (0)1580 755 700
E: helen@helenbratby.co.uk
www.helenbratby.co.uk

Pages 27 below right, 36,
43 above right, 50–51, 52
left, 53, 58, 61, 91 above
left, above centre and below
left, 95, 141, 142–143,
152–153.

Stine Busk
Munderingskompgniet
MDK
Ostbanegade 3 St.Th
DK-2100 Copenhagen
Denmark
T: +45 31 13 13 97
E: stinebusk@mail.dk

Pages 15, 18, 35, 37 above
right, 68 below left, 90
below centre, 90 right, 93
left, 102–103, 106 right,
107, 137 above left.

Debbie Johnson
Powder Blue – Styling Props
Locations
www.powder-blue.co.uk
E: Debbie@powder-blue.
co.uk
M: +44 (0)7790 474818

Endpapers, 26, 27 above
right, 37 below right,
52 right, 62, 63, 67 above
centre, 67 above right,
67 below, 68 above, 69,
70–74, 84, 92 right, 93
right, 104–105.

Jeanette Lunde
www.madeofrocks.com

Pages 3–5, 24 centre, 115
above right, 115 below left,
116 above right, 116 below,
118–119, 126–133.

An-Magritt Moen
Webshop: Pil & Bue
(Arrow & Bow)
www.pilbue.no

Pages 6 right, 7, 24 right,
34, 54, 55, 92 left, 98–101,
106 left.

Polly's Tearoom
(owned by Hanne Gran)
Storgata 20
1776 Halden
Norway
T: +47 919 12 379

Pages 42, 48 right, 82–83,
85, 110, 111, 115 below
centre, 120–123, 125.

Debi Treloar
www.debitreloar.com

Pages 13 centre, 14 right,
22, 29 left, 38, 39, 43
above left, 43 above centre,
43 below left, 43 below
centre, 60 right, 66,
76 above left, 76 below,
136 right, 139 above left.

Vintage Vacations
The Mission and The Scout
Hall are available for holiday
hire at
www.vintagevacations.co.uk

Pages 19, 27 above left, 28
left, 29 right, 37 below left,
44, 56, 57, 60 left, 94,
108–109, 136 left.

Index

A

accessories 13
ACR 23
amaranthus 92, 92
amaryllis 27, 29, 43, 74, 82, 115
Anthropologie 44, 45, 59, 139
antiques 82
apple decorations 124, 124
architectural features 66, 76, 78
armchairs 18
   faded grandeur 75
   homespun 42, 51, 56
   mid-century modern 20
   rustic 104
artwork 20, 98, 99, 128, 152
autumn-leaf garland 47
autumn love hearts 95, 95

B

baking 12
barns 96, 97, 97, 152–3
baskets 115
baubles 152
   patchwork tree baubles 143, 143
   vintage baubles 14, 122, 139, 139, 147
bed linen 30, 31
   homespun 58, 59, 60, 61
   winter 13, 20
bedrooms
   faded grandeur 72
   flooring 19
   homespun 58–61
   wallpaper 30, 31
beds 12, 59, 67, 70, 72
bell garlands 133, 133
berries
   berry wreaths 137
   displays 36, 37, 37, 43, 52, 52
blankets 19, 42, 50, 56
   crochet 60, 60, 61, 72
   knitted 12, 20, 20
   rustic 90, 91
   white 114, 115
bottles 52, 52, 126–7
boughs 37, 37
Bowness, Deborah 19, 20, 29, 30, 56

bundt tins/pans 12
bunting
   fairy light bunting 118, 119, 119
   felt bunting 143, 143

C

cafés 125
   as inspiration 82, 82, 83
cakes 12
candelabra 68, 100, 101
candleholders 77, 93
candles
   as colour interest 150, 151
   faded grandeur 68, 68, 69
   in jars 83, 116, 125
   moss candle arrangements 119, 119
   scented candles 24
   table decorations 13, 20, 119, 119, 148
   tealights 13, 20, 69, 115, 144, 144
   wreath decorations 147
candlesticks 80
Caravan 77
cards, Christmas 13, 14, 14, 145, 145
chairs 19, 20, 42, 67, 147
chandeliers 68
   chandelier decorations 52, 52
chocolate fruit and nut bundt cake 12
Christmas 134–51
   Christmas cards 13, 14, 145, 145
   Christmas trees 125, 138, 139
   wreaths 136–7, 152
cider, mulled 148, 148
cinnamon sticks 24, 92
cladding, wooden
   in hallways 45
   rustic 90, 101
   Scandi look 50, 51, 82, 83, 120, 121, 123
clothes lines 54
coat hooks 45
coffee tables 130
Cole & Son 30

colours
   colour pop party 150–1
   faded grandeur 73, 76
   rustic 90, 102
   whites 110–33
comforters see duvets
console tables 128
corsages 72
country Christmas 140–3
Cox and Cox 47, 59
crafting 13, 44
cupboards 56
curtains 13, 58, 114
cushions 13, 20, 20
   faded grandeur 67, 76, 76
   floral 18, 35, 99
   homespun 42, 43, 45, 47, 50, 51, 59, 60, 61
cutlery 145, 152

D

decorations 115
   autumn leaf garland 47
   baubles 14, 122, 139, 143, 147, 152
   chandelier decorations 52, 52
   Christmas tree 141
   fairy light bunting 118, 119, 119
   felt bunting 143, 143
   garlands 20, 47, 51, 60, 70, 95, 106, 107, 133
   gilded pear table decorations 81
   homespun 51
   lampshade garland 70
   painted apples 124, 124
   patchwork tree baubles 143, 143
   pine cone wall display 106, 106
   pom-pom garlands 60, 60
   rustic garland 106, 106, 107
   rustic-style 92, 94
   vintage decorations 43
   wall decorations 106, 106, 132
   window decorations 94, 94
dining rooms 23, 80, 148
dining tables 20, 147
   faded grandeur 80
   New Year's Eve settings 152, 153
   romantic whites 121

Diptyque 24, 68
dried fruit, chocolate fruit and nut bundt cake 12
drinks 13
duvets 20

E

Eames, Charles and Ray 98, 100, 101
eiderdowns 12, 20, 42, 70, 72
Ercol 98, 130
Etsy 44
eucalyptus 21, 24

F

fabrics 30, 43
faded grandeur 62–85
fairy lights 116, 118, 119, 119, 144
Farrow & Ball 23
felt bunting 143, 143
festive celebrations 134–53
festoon lights 116, 116, 151
Fine Little Day 20, 56, 91, 100, 101, 101
firelighters, pine cone 124, 124
fireplaces 12, 23
fires 12, 56, 139
flatware see cutlery
flooring 19, 42, 51
   homespun flooring 59
   white-painted flooring 114, 120
florals 26–37, 50, 58, 99
flowers 13, 21
   arrangements 27, 28–9, 32, 33, 43, 52, 52, 67, 148
   dried flowers 20
   garland decorations 133, 133
foliage arrangements 23, 52, 52
Folksy 44
frames, gilt 81
French inspiration 82, 83, 120–7
fruit 150, 151
furniture
   homespun 59
   paint effects 66
   retro 98, 98, 102, 109
   romantic whites 120
   Scandi look 51

G

garlands 20, 51, 133, 133
   autumn leaf garland 47

158 INDEX

autumn love hearts 95, *95*
lampshade garland 70
pom-pom garland 60, *60*
rustic garland 106, *106, 107*
gift tags 145, *145*
gifts, wrapping 14
gilding 80, 81
gilt frames 81
gold leaf 80, 81, *139*
grandeur, faded 62–85

H
hallways *74, 76*
headboards 60, *61*
Heart Vintage *84*
holiday retreats *108,* 109, *109*
homespun look 42–61
honesty seedpods *91*
hot chocolate 12
hot water bottles 12
hydrangea *32, 33, 67, 126–7*

I
IKEA 19, *20, 128*
incense sticks 24
industrial rustic 90
inspirations 9–37

J
jars 52, *52, 115, 125,* 144

K
kitchen tables *100,* 101
kitchens
  flooring 19
  homespun 48, *48, 49*
  rustic *105*
  studio kitchen *130*
knitting 13, *54*

L
lamps *51,* 129, *129*
lampshades
  homespun *43, 50, 52, 53,* 60, *61*
  lampshade garland 70
leaves
  autumn-leaf garland 47
  window decorations 94, *94*
Liberty London 76, *142*
lighting 13
  faded grandeur 68–71
  pendant lights 68, *100,* 101
  winter lighting 116–19

the Linen Works *59*
Linwood Fabrics 45
living areas 109, *109*
living rooms 19, 42, *75*
log cabins 56–7
logs 90, *91*

M
Mabel & Bird *20*
mantelpieces 14
marshmallows 12
matches *91*
mats 19
Mid-Century Modern *56,* 90, 98–101
mirrors *76, 85*
Mr Perswall 30, *31*
moss candle arrangements 119, *119*
mulled cider 13, 148, *148*
mulled wine 13

N
napkins *139*
natural Christmas 144–5
nature 20
  bringing indoors 92–5
New Year's Eve 152–3
nuts, chocolate fruit and nut bundt cake 12

O
opulence, understated 76
oranges, clove-studded 25

P
paintwork *21, 23*
paper chains *142*
parties 13, 97
  colour pop 150–1
  New Year's Eve 152–3
patchwork tree baubles 143, *143*
pears decorations 81, 124, *124*
pendant lights 68, *100,* 101
The People Shop 45
pine cones
  displays of 92, *93, 121, 122*
  pine cone firelighters 124, *124*
  pine cone wall display 106, *106*
  pine cone wreaths *137*
  and winter scents 24, *24*

plan chests *131*
The Plantation Rug Company 19, 139
plates *85, 91*
Plum & Ashby 24
pomanders 25, 139
posies 27
posters *131*
pots 20, *93, 123, 144, 152*

Q
quilts 12

R
retro style 98, *98, 102,* 109
Retro Sugar 152
Retro Villa 30
ribbon 14
romantic whites 120–7
rosemary 92
rugs *18,* 19, 20, *115*
rustic retreat 86–109

S
Scandi homespun look 51–5, *82, 83*
scents 24–5
scout hut *108,* 109, *109*
second-hand furniture 82
sewing 13
side tables *50*
smudge sticks 24, *24*
sofas 42, 51, 76, *130*
stools *50*
storage *43*
styling your home 19–23

T
table decorations
  gilded pear table decorations 81
  table settings 37, *37*
tables 42
  dining 20, 80, *121,* 147, 152, *153*
  kitchen *100,* 101
  rustic *103*
Talking Tables 150, 151, 152, *153*
tea canisters *48*
tealights 13, 20, *69, 115,* 144
textiles 20, 42, 90
textures
  faded grandeur 66–9, 76

homespun 42–3
rustic 90–1
whites 114–15
throws 12, 19, *59,* 114
tones
  faded grandeur 66–9
  homespun 42–3
  rustic 90–1, *98, 99*
  whites 114–15
traditional Christmas 146–8
trees 92
  Christmas trees *125, 138,* 139
  decorations 14, *141, 143, 143*
trims 76
True Grace 24, *150,* 151
twigs 92, *92, 121*

V
Valspar *21, 103, 105*
vases 20, *24, 27–8, 52, 52, 67, 122*
vignettes *84, 85*
vintage
  vintage Christmas 139
  vintage decorations 43
Vintage Vacations *108,* 109, *109*

W
wall charts 33, *33, 34*
wall displays, pine cone 106, *106*
Wallography 33, *33*
wallpaper 14, 26, 30, 66
walls
  exposed plaster 66, 70
  panel walls 102
  wall decorations 106, *106, 132*
  wood clad 45, 50, 51, *82, 83,* 90, 101, *120, 121, 123*
whites 110–33
window decorations 94, *94*
wine, mulled 13
wood, dark 102, 147
wood burning stoves 50, 56
work spaces 128–31
wrapping gifts 14
  wrapping paper *145*
wreaths 14, *131,* 136–7, *139*
  autumn love hearts 95, *95*
  candle wreaths 147
  Christmas wreaths 136–7, *152*

I would like to dedicate this book to my grandparents, Doreen and Robert Howard-Baylis and Lilian and Ronald Lake.

Acknowledgments

I would like to thank my publishers, Ryland Peters & Small, and everyone who worked hard to produce this book with me. I'm delighted to have worked with you on six books so far. Huge thanks to my friend Debi Treloar – your photography is always amazing and I love working with you. I really enjoyed travelling through Norway with you and in particular experiencing a traditional Norwegian Christmas dinner together!

Once again I went to some amazing locations and homes while shooting this book, so a huge thank you to all the home and location owners who made Debi and I feel welcome and let me style them up. My highlights were Debbie Johnson's Faded Grandeur space, Jeanette Lunde's Winter Whites Scandi studio, Helen Bratby's old barn and home with tons of inspiring handmade details and Anmagritt Moen's rustic Norwegian house and barn. Thanks to Debbie Johnson, Katy Fletcher, Annabella Daughtry, Sarah Prall and Rosie Martindill for assisting me on the photoshoots – I really appreciated your help.

Also a huge thank you to all the companies who sent me lovely winter home accessories, paint and wallpaper, especially Cox and Cox, Talking Tables, Deborah Bowness, Ikea, ACR heat products, True Grace, Mr Perswall, The Plantation Rug Company, and Dulux, Farrow & Ball and Valspar for the paint. Plus another thanks to Debbie Johnson and Sarah Prall for the amazing props.

Big thanks also to my blogging and Facebook friends, followers on Twitter, Instagram & Pinterest – I'd love to see some of your Winter styling if you've been inspired by any of my ideas in this book. @selinalake #selinalakewinterliving

Last but not least to my lovely family, who I've spent many a cold winter's day with. I've enjoyed our freezing days at Kempton Park on Boxing Day, blustery winter walks at Hengistbury Head, Christmases at Crathes (and now Manor Road) and mum's surprise hot water bottles, which warmed my bed up for me when I was little. Thanks Mum and Dad and my husband Dave, who makes the best, cosiest fires at home. Love You X